IOT-BASED DOOR ACCESS CONTROL VIA WEB APPLICATION

IOT-BASED DOOR ACCESS CONTROL VIA WEB APPLICATION

Felix Ndudirim Stanley

ELIVA PRESS

ISBN: 978-99949-8-721-4

Cover Design: Eliva Press
Cover Image: Ingimage
Email: info@elivapress.com
Website: www.elivapress.com

This Eliva Press imprint is published by the registered company Eliva Press Global Ltd. part of Eliva Press S.R.L. Publishing Group

The registered company address is: Pope Hennessy Street Level 2, Hennessy Tower Port Louis, Mauritius
Eliva Press S.R.L. Publishing Group address is: Bulevardul Moscova 21, Chisinau, Moldova, Europe

DEVELOPMENT OF AN IOT-BASED DOOR ACCESS CONTROL VIA WEB APPLICATION

BY

AUTHOR: FELIX NDUDIRIM STANLEY

CO AUTHOR 1: ENYITE SAMUEL

CO AUTHOR 2: EZEOFOR JOSEPH

EMAIL ADDRESS: felixndudirim@gmail.com

TABLE OF CONTENT

ABSTRACT

The Development of an IOT-based door access control Via web application entails the remote monitoring technology which confirm visitor identity and to control Door accessibility has been reported in this study. Smart home security control system has become indispensable in daily life. Over the years, house owners find it difficult to curb the rate of theft and burglary which was initiated by arm robbers in breaking through their homes. The footage of such incidents cannot be found anywhere and hence those culprits cannot be brought to book. It was a major challenge for aged parents to be taken proper care of, in the absence of other people. This study describes the implementation and deployment of an internet based camera control system and accessibility restriction into a home environment for authenticated people only. The system features the use of ESP32 CAM board for streaming video through the use of a non-static IP-address protocol to connected android devices for video correspondence. A web application with buttons to enable remote opening and closing from anywhere in the world has also been designed in the study. A 12V electromagnetic door lock module to operate the door accessibility has been designed and developed. The actuator system is built into the door mechanically to aid remote control over the internet. In the system implementation, when visitor face is recognized at door through the camera module interfaced to the ESP32 CAM, the home owner or concerned authority can then control the system by remotely granting access to the visitor or by refusing to grant access to the visitor. Developing an IOT-based access control has really helped in all-round monitoring and access control of users' door and thereby reduce the challenges faced by individuals who are not residing within the premises.

CHAPTER ONE

INTRODUCTION

1.1. Background to the Study

A door is a panel which covers an entrance into a building. This panel could be made of wood, metal, glass, plastic material, aluminum or a combination of these materials. Doors make ingress into or egress from a building, room, or vehicle easier to manage. The panel may be moved in various ways (at angles away from the frame, by sliding on a plane parallel to the frame, by folding in angles on a parallel plane, or by spinning along an axis at the center of the frame) to allow or prevent ingress or egress. Much beyond providing and restricting access to defined spaces in a building, doors can also fulfill added requirements of ensuring some level of privacy by preventing unwanted attention from outsiders, of separating areas with different functions, of allowing light to pass into and out of a space, of controlling ventilation or air drafts so that interiors may be more effectively heated or cooled, of dampening noise, and of blocking the spread of fire.

According to Alkar and Buhur, the need for automation has come to stay and this date back to 1500 years when the first water pump for metal working rolling mills for coinage strips was developed from then till date the automation world has continued to grow tremendously. Automation is the art of making processes or machines self-acting or self-moving, it also pertains to the technique of making a device, machine, process or procedure more fully automatic, it is a self-controlling or self-moving process.

The demand for automations and automatic systems in the industrial and commercial space is an ever increasing one. This is due to the need to replace some routine actions which are managed and executed manually with automatic methods. One of such routine chore or procedure is the opening and closing of doors manually. In the commercial and industrial environment, this action is usually executed by a doorman or a gate keeper. The maintenance and payment of these gatekeepers or doormen at various doorways may lead to a higher cost of running such establishments (Adewuyi 2013). The process of opening and closing of a door is also detrimental to the health and wellbeing of the doorman. This is as a result of him/her having to stand for long hours in order to ensure that the door is opened and closed for persons to go through. This might lead to health challenges such as generalized body pain, waist pain and fatigue. There is therefore the need for door systems which could open and close automatically. This study presents a design whereby, a home owner can verify the identity of any individual requesting access to his/her building and can decide to grant or refuse access remotely. Thus there is no need for a door keeper or guard as the system self protects the entrance. The system is designed to be independent of grid power supply as it is powered by a 12V, 7.2AH battery.

1.2. Statement of Problem

Home security has always been an issue for people, especially for people who are not always available at their home; children, people of old aged, and physically challenged people. Incidents like robbery, stealing, or unwanted entrance can happen unexpectedly. This can cause issue to people who are not convenient to encounter such problems. Different type security system had been invented before the IoT era, such as password-based system or smart card-based system. The system designed in this study leverages on IoT for improving home security. Especially security around doors or entrance points in buildings such that it provides remote identification and then access control, geared towards checkmating the problem of security breach or unauthorized entry.

1.3. Aim and Objectives

The aim of this study is to develop an IoT based Door Access Control capable of offering access control via Online Web application. The following objectives were used to achieve the project aim:

- To design and fabricate a 3 feet wooden door
- To design the control circuitry using ESP32 CAM, ESP 32 and electromechanical actuator for door self-locking and self-unlocking.
- To program and configure the ESP CAM for video streaming

- To design a web application with an authorization/ OPEN button for unlocking the door remotely from anywhere in the world.
- To interface the door electronic circuit to the web application.

1.4. Significance of the Study

The design and fabrication of the proximity door proposed in this study would boost the implementation of IoT based automatic access control in residential homes and small commercial buildings.

The fabrication and implementation of an IoT based automatic door would ease mobility through doorways for disabled persons, eliminating the need to manually open and close doors. The application of such a door system would immensely benefit industrial and commercial buildings as it would minimize the need for multiple doormen thus benefiting such an establishment financially.

1.5. Scope of the Study

This study covers the design of a web application based IoT door system to carry out remote identification and access control. The study implementation is done over a 3feet sized door and not an actual door size. A micro-processor ATMEGA 328 Board is equally used to interface with the ESP Camera Board and a 12v DC Lock actuator which opens when energized and closes when a low signal is sent to it. A web application is designed as a key to send a high signal to the ESP 32 Board which opens the actuator whenever the door needs to be opened.

1.6 Report Organization

This project report is divided into five chapters; 1, 2, 3, 4 & 5

Chapter One discusses the background of the study, aims, objectives, significance, and the scope of this study.

Chapter Two; a general literature review was carried out on the history, evolution and development of intelligent security doors and a review of similar works carried out by other researchers.

Chapter Three focuses on the materials used and the fabrication procedures employed in the fabrication of the IoT based access control door system.

Chapter Four results are obtained, discussed and analyzed in this chapter.

Chapter Five here, general conclusions are drawn on the work carried out in this project and recommendations made for future work.

CHAPTER TWO

LITERATURE REVIEW

2.1. Historical Background

The earliest doors in records are those represented in the paintings of some Egyptian tombs, in which they are shown as single or double doors, each in a single piece of wood. Doors were once believed to be the literal doorway to the afterlife, and some doors leading to important places included designs of the afterlife. In Egypt, where the climate is intensely dry, there would be no fear of their warping, but in other countries it would be necessary to frame them, which according to Vitruvius as cited by (Howard, 2013) was done with stiles and rails the spaces enclosed being filled with panels (tympana) let into grooves made in the stiles and rails. The stiles were the vertical boards, one of which, tenoned or hinged, is known as the hanging stile, the other as the middle or meeting stile. The horizontal cross pieces are the top rail, bottom rail, and middle or intermediate rails.

The most ancient doors were made of timber, such as those referred to in the Biblical depiction of King Solomon's temple being in olive wood, which were carved and overlaid with gold. The doors dwelt upon in Homer would appear to have been cased in silver or brass. Besides olive wood, elm, cedar, oak and cypress were used. A 5,000-year-old door has been found by archaeologists in Switzerland (I Kings vi. 31-35).

All ancient doors were hung by pivots at the top and bottom of the hanging stile which worked in sockets in the lintel and sill, the latter being always in some hard stone such as basalt or granite. Those found at Nippur by Dr. Hilprecht dating from 2000 B.C. were in dolerite. The tenons of the gates at Balawat were sheathed with bronze (now in the British Museum). These doors or gates were hung in two leaves, each about 8 ft 4 in (2.54 m) wide and 27 ft (8.2 m) high; they were encased with bronze bands or strips, 10 in. high, covered with repouss decoration of figures, etc. The wood doors would seem to have been about 3 in. thick, but the hanging stile was over 14 inches (360 mm) diameter. Other sheathings of various sizes in bronze have been found, which proves this to have been the universal method adopted to protect the wood pivots. (Ashis and Aman, 2014). In the Hauran in Syria, where timber is scarce the doors were made in stone, and one measuring 5 ft 4 in (1.63 m) by 2 ft 7 in (0.79 m) is in the British Museum; the band on the meeting stile shows that it was one of the leaves of a double door. At Kuffeir near Bostra in Syria, Burckhardt found stone doors, 9 to 10 ft (3.0 m). high, being the entrance doors of the town (Dennis, 2017).

The ancient Greek and Roman doors were single doors, double doors, triple doors, sliding doors or folding doors, in the last case the leaves were hinged and folded back. In Eumachia, is a painting of a door with three leaves. In the tomb of Theron at Agrigentum there is a single four-panel door carved in stone. In the Blundell collection is a bas-relief of a temple with double doors, each leaf with five panels. Among existing examples, the bronze doors in the church of SS. Cosmas and Damiano, in Rome, are important examples of Roman metal work of the best period; they are in two leaves, each with two panels, and are framed in bronze. Those of the Pantheon are similar in design, with narrow horizontal panels in addition, at the top, bottom and middle. Two other bronze doors of the Roman period are in the Lateran Basilica.

The oldest door in England can be found in Westminster Abbey and dates from 1050. In England in the 17th century the door panels were raised with bolection or projecting moldings, sometimes richly carved, round them; in the 18th century the moldings worked on the stiles and rails were carved with the egg and tongue ornament.

The Greek scholar Heron of Alexandria created the earliest known automatic door in the 1st century AD during the era of Roman Egypt. The first foot-sensor-activated automatic door was made in China during the reign of Emperor Yang of Sui (r. 604–618), who had one installed for his royal library. The first automatic gate operators were later created in 1206 by Arab inventor Al-Jazari. (Needham, 2015).

2.1.1 Types of Door mechanism

A. Hinged doors

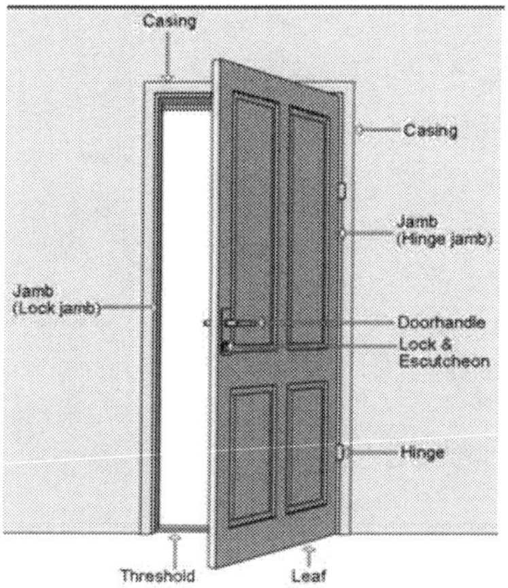

Most doors are hinged along one side to allow the door to pivot away from the doorway in one direction, but not the other. The axis of rotation is usually vertical. In some cases, such as hinged garage doors, the axis may be horizontal, above the door opening. Doors can be hinged so that the axis of rotation is not in the plane of the door to reduce the space required on the side to which the door opens. This requires a mechanism so that the axis of rotation is on the side other than that in which the door opens. This is sometimes the case in trains or airplanes, such as for the door to the toilet, which opens inward (Garvin, 1997).

B. Swing door. This has special single-action hinges that allow it to open either outwards or inwards, and is usually sprung to keep it closed.

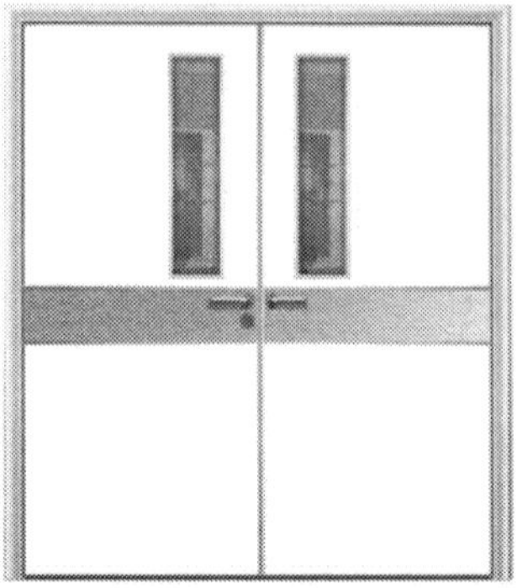

C. **Self-bolting door** has special hinges that permit the panel leaf to move laterally, so that the door itself becomes a giant bolt for better security. The self-bolting door principle can be used both for hinged doors as for rotating doors, as well as up-and-over doors (in the latter case, the bolts are then placed at top and bottom rather than at the sides) (Nicholson, 2014).

D. **French doors** are derived from an original French design called the casement door. It is a door with lites where all or some panels would be in a casement door. A French door traditionally has a moulded panel at the bottom of the door. It is called a French window when used in a pair as double-leaved doors with large glass panels in each door leaf, and in which the doors may swing out (typically) as well as in (Henley, 2016).

E. A **Dutch door** or stable door consists of two halves. The top half operates independently from the bottom half. A variant exists in which opening the top part separately is possible, but because the lower part has a lip on the inside, closing the top part, while leaving the lower part open (Chai, 2009).

F. A **garden door** resembles a French window (with lights), but is more secure because only one door is operable. The hinge of the operating door is next to the adjacent fixed door and the latch is located at the wall opening jamb rather than between the two doors or with the use of an espagnolette bolt (Garvin, 1997).

G. Sliding doors

It is often useful to have doors which slide along tracks, often for space or aesthetic considerations.

H. A **bypass door** is a door unit that has two or more sections. The doors can slide in either direction along one axis on parallel overhead tracks, sliding past each other. They are most commonly used in closets, in order to access one side of the closet at a time. The doors in a bypass unit will overlap slightly when viewed from the front, in order not to have a visible gap between them.

I. Doors which slide inside a wall cavity are called **pocket doors**. This type of door is used in tight spaces where privacy is also required. The door slab is mounted to roller and a track at the top of the door and slides inside a wall. Sliding glass doors are common in many houses, particularly as an entrance to the backyard. Such doors are also popular for use for the entrances to commercial structures, although they are not counted as fire exit doors. The door that moves is called the "active leaf", while the door that remains fixed is called the "inactive leaf" (Patil 2012).

J. Rotating doors

A **revolving door** has several wings or leaves, generally four, radiating from a central shaft, forming compartments that rotate about a vertical axis.

A revolving door allows people to pass in both directions without colliding, and forms an airlock maintaining a seal between inside and out (Howard, 2011).

K. A **pivot door**, instead of hinges, is supported on a bearing some distance away from the edge, so that there is more or less of a gap on the pivot side as well as the opening side. In some cases the pivot is central, creating two equal openings (Alkar et al, 20014).

L. **High-speed door**

A **high-speed door** is a very fast door some with opening speeds of up to 4 m/s, mainly used in the industrial sector where the speed of a door has an effect on production logistics, temperature and pressure control. high-speed clean room doors are used in pharmaceutical industries for the special curtain and stainless steel frames. They guarantee the tightness of all accesses.

The powerful high-speed doors have a smooth surface structure and no protruding edges. Therefore, they can be easily cleaned and depositing of particles is largely excluded (Edward et al, 2013).

High-speed doors are made to handle a high number of openings, generally more than 200,000 a year. They need to be built with heavy-duty parts and counterbalance systems for speed enhancement and emergency opening function. The door curtain was originally made of PVC, but was later also developed in aluminium and acrylic glass sections. High Speed refrigeration and cold room doors with excellent insulation values was also introduced with the Green and Energy saving requirements (Jonathan and Michael, 2014).

In North America, the Door and Access Systems Manufacturing Association (DASMA) according to NBS GCR 78-156, BOSTI of 1979 defines high-performance doors as non-residential, powered doors, characterized by rolling, folding, sliding or swinging action, that are either high-cycle (minimum 100 cycles/day) or high-speed (minimum 20 inches(508 mm)/second), and two out of three of the following: made-to-order for exact size and custom features, designed to be able to withstand equipment impact (break-away if accidentally hit by vehicle) or designed to sustain heavy usage with minimal maintenance.

2.2 Empirical Reviews

(Halliru, 2020) noted that home security system has been very poor due to the increased rate of intrusion in recent years. His research projects consisted of a smart door locking system which provides a great solution to improve the home safety and management of doors. He used the Arduino IDE software and a

Bluetooth module hc-05 to connect between a smartphone, the microcontroller and the door lock were to give an easy access to authorized persons. The design was such that the person with the authority to open the door can have access within their fingertips by installing the required application which has open/close button. A screen shot of the smartphone used is shown below

Figure 2.1: Access door Bluetooth application (Halliru, 2020)

The hc-05 served as a receiver and transmitter but also communicates with the microcontroller which serves as a processing unit in this project and decides whether the password entered by the user is right or wrong and then send the servo motor to either open or close the door. If the password is right the user can have access to the door and when the password is wrong the user will have no access whatsoever. His approach was able to enhance the safety and security of main entrance doors.

(Shuhada , 2012) also put forward a study presenting the development of a door access system including many different features from as simple as keypad to as complex as using smart cards and biometrics. The Door Access System is developed to overcome the issue of upgrading and maintenaning the system which happens to be a challenge in the existing systems. The study discusses on the door access system using Arduino MCU board, the project had two featured inputs, which are keypad and fingerprint scanner. While the outputs are magnetic switch, indicator, LCD display and a siren. A process diagram of how the system was designed is presented below.

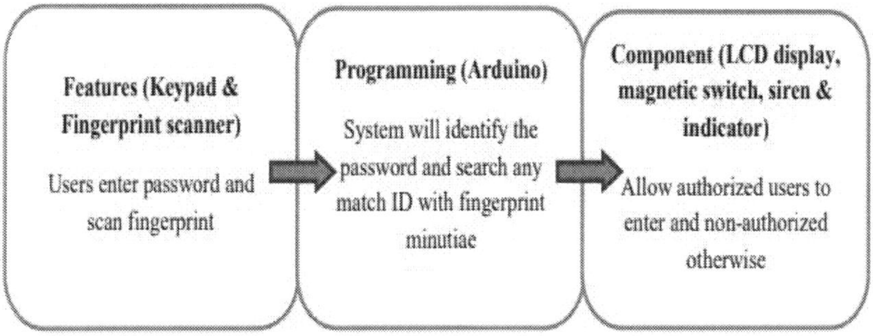

Figure 2.2: Keypad access door Process flow chart (Shuhada, 2012)

Interfacing all inputs and outputs with Arduino produced accurate results in accessing the door based on the accuracy results obtained by performing a test on five individuals with four different fingerprints each person. The entered password using keypad and obtained by scanning fingerprint are clarified as inputs, while the output is the result displayed on LCD display.

(Zungeru and Abraham 2013), designed an automatic digital sliding door with room light control. This system consisted of two transmitting infrared diodes and two receiving photodiodes. The first one was for detecting persons coming in and the second one was for persons going out of the room. The photodiodes were connected to comparators, which give a lower output when the beam is broken and high output when transmitting normally. The general operation of the work and performance was dependent on the presence of an intruder entering through the door and how close he/she was to the door. The door opens automatically but in a case as it was completely reliant on grid power supply. This makes it inapplicable in countries such as Nigeria where power supply is epileptic.

In the work of (Ashis and Aman, 2014), an automated door was developed, designed to slide on appropriate slider and worked on pneumatic air pressure. It consisted of two IR proximity sensors which sense the presence of obstacle in their way. The pneumatic actuator was controlled by the codes in the Arduino. The cylinders retracted when the obstruction is detected by the IR sensors thus opening the door and expands when the obstacle has been detected by the second IR sensor located on the other side. This pneumatic operation was controlled by suitable electro-pneumatic circuit. Their design was able to address the challenge of developing a low cost automated door based on proximity sensing but had no form of locking mechanism thus making it not ideal for implementation in homes and commercial buildings.

In the work of (Primus, 2015), a low cost automatic gate system was developed. Their design made use of the IR sensor TSOP1736, An Arduino Uno R3, MD10C Motor Driver, a 12V DC power supply and DC Motor (Power window) 12V as the main actuator of the system. The operation of the system was based on the signal sent from the IR sensor to the Arduino microcontroller. Upon approaching the gate, a button is pressed causing the IR sensor to send a pulse signals to the controller board. This signals when received by the Arduino Uno is interpreted and the DC motor is turn on, pulling the gate open. This system was not completely autonomous as it requires an individual to manually initiate the opening and closing of the gate by pressing a push button.

2.3 Knowledge Gap

From the literature reviewed, the system have been made to design and fabricate an automated door with an Internet of things based system. The automatic doors developed by other researches so far make use of Infra-red remote lock or key lock.

This study seeks to improve on the works of other researchers by implementing an IoT based system in an access control door. This is done in order to facilitate and encourage the implementation of IoT based access doors in residential, smaller commercial buildings such as retail shops, restaurants, as the door developed in this work operates independent of grid power supply.

CHAPTER THREE

MATERIALS AND METHODS

3.1 Design Approach

The design of the IoT based access control door system is presented in this chapter. All design parameters involving the web interface, the internet protocol as well as the chassis and hardware design are all presented and discussed in subsequent subsections of this chapter. The system presented in this study is essentially an access control based IoT door system embedded with video stream features and capable of achieving remote control from anywhere in the world. The ESP32 CAM board as well as the custom ESP32 board itself is the boards used in this system design. The ESP 32 CAM board provides video surveillance over a LAN while the ESP 32 custom board serves as a web server to link the hardware to the web application running on line. In the system implementation, it is assumed that the home owner is able to get clear video footages of the identity of the individual requiring access to the building before carrying out a remote "OPEN" action from to either grant or refuse access. The system block diagram is presented in figure 3.1 below.

The two controller boards employed in the system design are:

- ESP32 custom controller board
- ESP32 Camera board

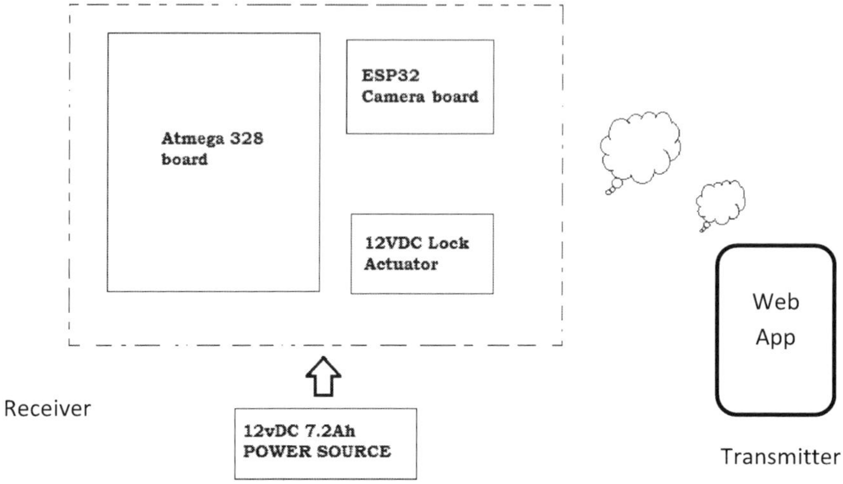

Figure 3.1: System Block diagram

3.1.1 ESP32 CAM board

The ESP32-CAM is built using the ESP32-S module as a foundation therefore it shares the same system specifications as its ancestor being the ESP32 board. The board is built to have an onboard camera interface for the camera module. The camera module receives power and signal inflow from the ESP32 board. In the design, the ESP board is programmed separately to connect to a local area network and stream video footage from the traffic unit to any internet enabled device connected to the LAN. The ESP32 was selected because it runs on ultra-low power consumption and can run several types of proprietary software. The board's schematic diagram and its dimensions are found below as shown in figure 3.2.

(a)

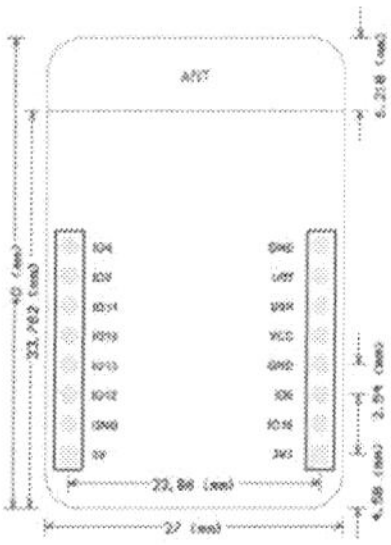

(b)

Figure 3.2(a) Diagram of ESP32 CAM **Figure 3.2(b) Form-factor of ESP32 CAM**

Table 1. Specifications of the ESP32 CAM board

Symbol	Parameter	Min	Typ	Max	Unit
VDDA, VDD3P3_RTC 1 VDD3P3, VDD_SDIO (3.3 V mode) 2	Voltage applied to power supply pins per power domain	2.3	3.3	3.6	V
VDD3P3_CPU	Voltage applied to power supply pin	1.8	3.3	3.6	V
IV DD	Current delivered by external power supply	0.5	-	-	A
T 3	Operating temperature	–40	-	125	°C

The ESP32 CAM was chosen to provide the video streaming requirement because the controller is based on a 32-bit CPU with a frequency of up to 240MHz. It has a built-in 520 KB SRAM with an external 4M PSRAM. It has a combined 802.11b/g/n Wi-Fi + Bluetooth/BLE SoC module. It supports image WiFI upload and Embedded Lwip and FreeRTOS. There is an onboard voltage regulator IC and a PSRAM Chip, so in cases of unregulated supply voltages to the system, the ESP32 CAM board offers self-protect features.

Also, the board has a single reset button which is useful during tests, unlike existing camera boards that require uploading a sketch to be flashed or rested. The board's architecture is provided in figure 3.3

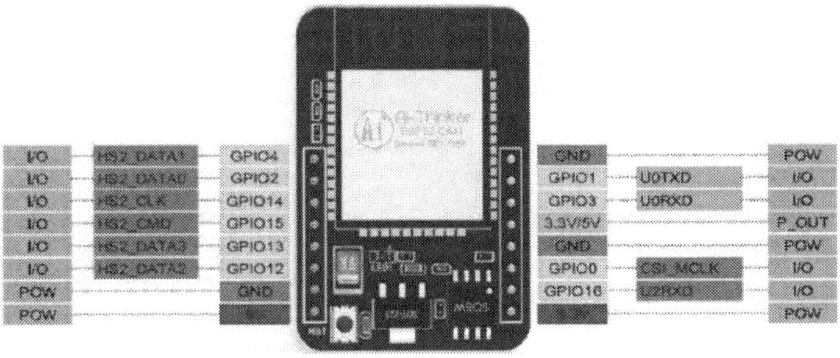

Figure 3.3: ESP32 CAM board schematic and architectural layout

3.1.2 ESP32 custom controller board

The ESP32 Development Board gives the full capabilities of both a superior microcontroller and an internet module all at once, which makes it the ideal choice for the implementation of an IoT based access control and monitoring system. It is economical, as it performs efficiently in the full range of requirements for both a microcontroller and an internet module while reducing cost; hence it was chosen to support the ESP32 CAM in designing the electronic circuitry. The ESP board serves as a web server for the web application running on the internet. Although the configuration of the ESP32 CAM and the ESP32 custom controller boards are quite similar, they are not the same as used in this study and design. The pin configuration of the ESP32 custom board is available in table 3.2 below.

Table 2. Showing Pin Configuration of the ESP32 (ESP32-2, 2020)

Pin Category	**Pin Name**	**Details**
Power	Micro-USB, 3.3V, 5V, GND	Micro-USB: ESP32 can be powered through USB port 5V: Regulated 5V can be supplied to this pin which is we be again regulated to 3.3V by on board regulator, to power the board. 3.3V: Regulated 3.3V can be supplied to this pin to power the board. GND: Ground pins
Enable	En	The pin and the button resets the microcontroller.
Analog Pins	ADC1_0 to ADC1_5 and ADC2_0 to ADC2_9	Used to measure analog voltage in the range of 0-3.3V. 12-bit 18 Channel ADC
DAC pins	DAC1 and DAC2	Used for Digital to analog Conversion

Input/Output Pins	GPIO0 to GPIO39	Totally 39 GPIO pins, can be used as input or output pins. 0V (low) and 3.3V (high). But pins 34 to 39 can be used as input only
Capacitive Touch pins	T0 to T9	These 10 pins can be used a touch pins normally used for capacitive pads
RTC GPIO pins	RTCIO0 to RTCIO17	These 18 GPIO pins can be used to wake up the ESP32 from deep sleep mode.
Serial	Rx, Tx	Used to receive and transmit TTL serial data.
External Interrupts	All GPIO	Any GPIO can be use to trigger an interrupt.
PWM	All GPIO	16 independent channel is available for PWM any GPIO can be made to work as PWM though software
VSPI	GPIO23 (MOSI), GPIO19(MISO), GPIO18(CLK) and GPIO5 (CS)	Used for SPI-1 communication.
HSPI	GPIO13 (MOSI), GPIO12(MISO), GPIO14(CLK) and GPIO15 (CS)	Used for SPI-2 communication.

IIC	GPIO21(SDA), GPIO22(SCL)	Used for I2C communication.
AREF	AREF	To provide reference voltage for input voltage.

Rui Santos and Sara Santos 2018

3.3 Development of Web application server with ESP32

A web application is required to run online as the door is to be controlled from anywhere in the world. Since the web application must require a server present in the hardware to handshake both the web application and the hardware together, the ESP is configured to serve as a web server because it offers on-board Wi-Fi connectivity features.

3.3.1 Building the Web server request-response

A Request-response is required in the design to create a message exchange pattern, in which a requestor (the home owner's browser) sends a request message to a replier system (the ESP32 present in the hardware) that receives and processes the request, and returns a message in response. A visual representation of the requestor replier system is illustrated in figure 3.4 below.

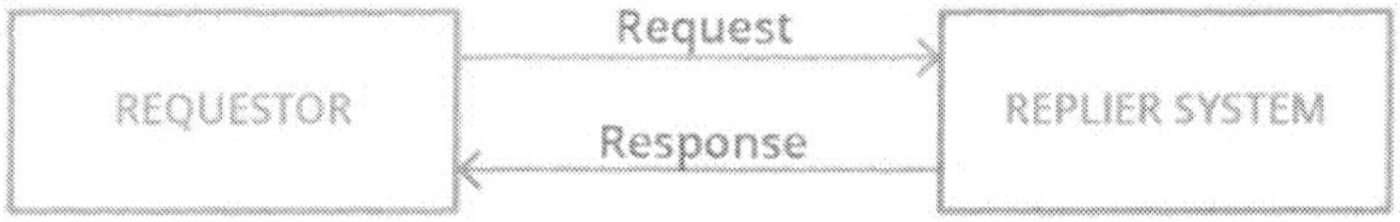

Figure 3.4: visual representation of the requestor replier protocol

3.3.2 Enabling LAN connectivity on the ESP32 through IP Address

In order to achieve wireless streaming of video feeds, the ESP is configured so as to be able to join a specific local area network using a particular ip address, SSID and password. Usually, the IP address is a numerical label assigned to each device connected to a computer network. It is a series of four values separated by periods with each value ranging from 0 to 255. The Arduino integrated development environment forms a complete suite for this configuration. We upload a sketch to search and connect to a given SSID. Thus, all devices connected to that host's ip address are part of the local network and thus can receive video footages from the camera. A visual representation of this network setup and configuration is presented in figure 3.5.

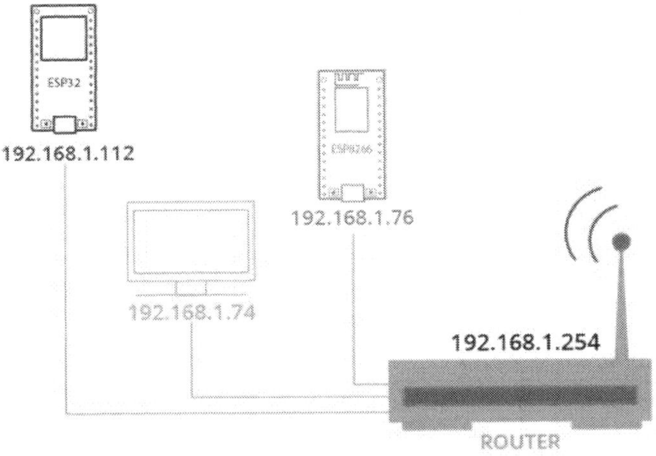

Figure 3.5: Visual representation of I.P Address LAN setup and configuration

3.4 Power supply

The power supply system of this project is very basic and without complexities. This is because the project will be powered by DC source, which eliminates the need for rectifying and filtering which would have been needed had it been AC. A 12V DC battery serves as the power supply for the entire project.

Fig.6: The 12V DC power source used for the project

The 12V is sufficient to power the linear actuator since the actuator itself is a 12/24V DC actuator. However, the microcontroller can only be powered by not more than 5V. This makes it necessary to regulate the power supplied to the microcontroller.

3.5 Isolation relays

The relay is responsible for interfacing the actuator, the power supply and the driving intelligence (code written on the microcontroller) together. The relay driver is used to isolate both the controlling and the controlled device.

The relay is an electromagnetic device, which consists of solenoid, moving contacts (switch) and restoring spring and consumes comparatively large amount of power. Hence it is possible for the interface IC to drive the relay satisfactorily. To enable this, a driver circuitry, which will act as a buffer circuit, is to be incorporated between them. The driver circuitry senses the presence of a "high" level at the input and drives the relay from another voltage source. Hence the relay is used to switch the electrical supply to the appliances.

Fig. 7: A relay driver circuit

The relay of choice is the SRD-05VDC relay circuit. It runs off a minimum of 5V and most controllers can easily drive it. The circuit is optically isolated from the relay, so the ESP controller is protected from voltage spikes and surges. It does this by shining light across a gap to a sensor. No electrically conductive items cross this gap.

- Relay Coil Voltage: 5V

- Logic Voltage: 5V (logic low activates relay)
- Relay Current: 10amp
- Relay Voltage: 250VAC or 30VDC

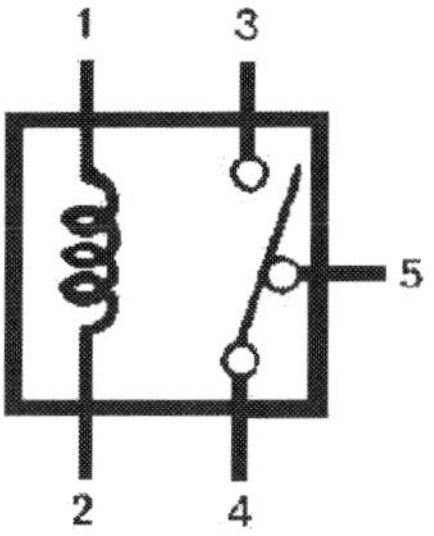

Fig.8: Diagrammatic representation of a relay

The relay system circuit diagram is presented in figure 3.9

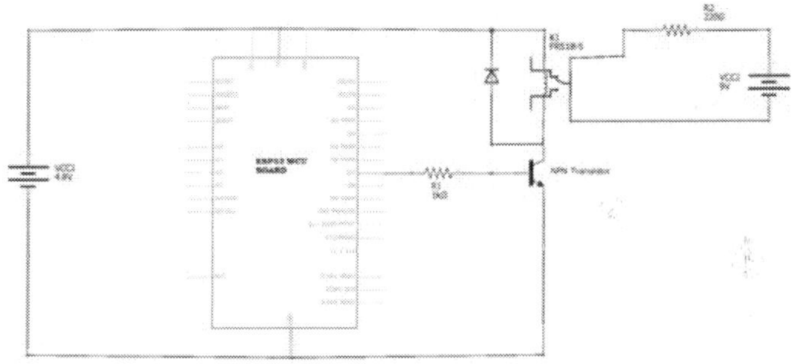

Figure 3.9: Relay system circuit diagram

3.6 Electromechanical Locking Actuator system

A simple electromechanical lock system actuator was used in the design to enable self-lock and self-open. The ESP controller is unable to source the operation power required to drive the actuator, thus it is powered through a 5V relay module. Information about the relay module used is provided in progressive subsection. The pictorial view of the actuator is presented in figure

3.10. The specifications of the solenoid lock module used in this work are given in table 3.3.

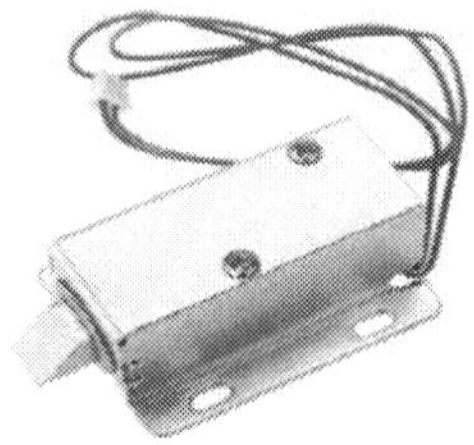

Figure 3.10: Pictorial view of actuator

Table 3.3: Technical Specifications of Solenoid Door Lock Module

S/N	Parameter	Specification
1	Operating voltage	12V DC
2	Activation Time	1-10 seconds long activation
3	Weight	147.71g
4	Unlocking Time	1s
5	Starting Current	650mA

3.7 Mechanical Power Output of the Actuator

This is the mechanical power produced by the actuator in order to drive a given load. This power is defined in watts. In order to get mechanical power out of an electric linear actuator, it's necessary to put electrical power into the system. Mechanical power output is calculated using the expression in equation 3.1.

Mechanical Power, P_o(W)

$$P_o = F \times V \qquad 3.1$$

$$F = m \times a \qquad 3.2$$

Where:

F= force (N).

V= Velocity (m/s).

m= mass of load (kg).

a= Acceleration of the actuator (m/s^2).

Electrical power, P_i (W).

$$P_i = E \times I \qquad 3.3$$

Where:

E= voltage (V).

I= current (A).

3.7.1 Moment applied on the Electric Pneumatic actuator

When electric linear actuators are in operation, moment loads occur due to gravity applied to the load and the acceleration of the load. Because moment loads have great influence on the service life of actuators, it is essential to make sure that they are determined and within the actuator specifications.

$$M_p = (m \cdot g \cdot L) + (m \cdot \alpha \cdot L) \qquad 3.4$$

Where:

M_p= Pitching direction moment applied on the linear actuator.

L= Overhung distance (m).

m= Mass of Load (door) (Kg).

α= Operating acceleration of the actuator (m/s^2).

g= acceleration due to gravity (m/s^2).

3.7.2 Thrust

Thrust is the amount if force required in moving a mass a given distance within a given time. This is calculated by summing up all the forces acting on the mass. These forces generally fall within the following four categories:

Gravity is important when something is being raised or lowered in a system. Lifting a mass vertically is one example, as is sliding something on an incline.

Friction forces exist in almost all systems and must be considered.

Applied forces are the forces that act on the mass other than friction, gravity, and the actuator's thrust.

Actuator thrust is the required actuator force, and is what we need to determine.

$$\Sigma F = m \times a \qquad 3.5$$

$$F_{actuator} - F_{applied} - F_{friction} - F_{gravity} = ma = \left(\frac{W_t}{g}\right) a \qquad 3.6$$

$$F_{actuator} = \left(\frac{W_t}{g}\right) a + F_{applied} + F_{friction} + F_{gravity} \qquad 3.7$$

Where:

$$W_t = W_{load} + W_{actuator} \qquad 3.8$$

$$F_{friction} = \mu WL\cos\theta \qquad 3.9$$

$$F_{gravity}=WL\sin\theta \quad 3.10$$

3.9 Software Development

The intelligence of the controller is written using C++ programming language with SPI protocol over the Arduino IDE (Integrated Development Environment) which converts the C++ code (.cpp) to machine code (hex) which the controller understands.

The program is developed such that the only the web based button can grant access. The 32-BIT ESP32 board, when connected to the internet is in a read state on GPIO Pin 21, if a digital HIGH is detected, the relay switches and triggers the solenoid lock to unlock for 5 seconds. Access is granted by the web based interface, after the visual data from the ESP32 CAM has been examined and the decision to grant access made by triggering the online button. The program controlling the IOT based access control door is presented in the appendix.

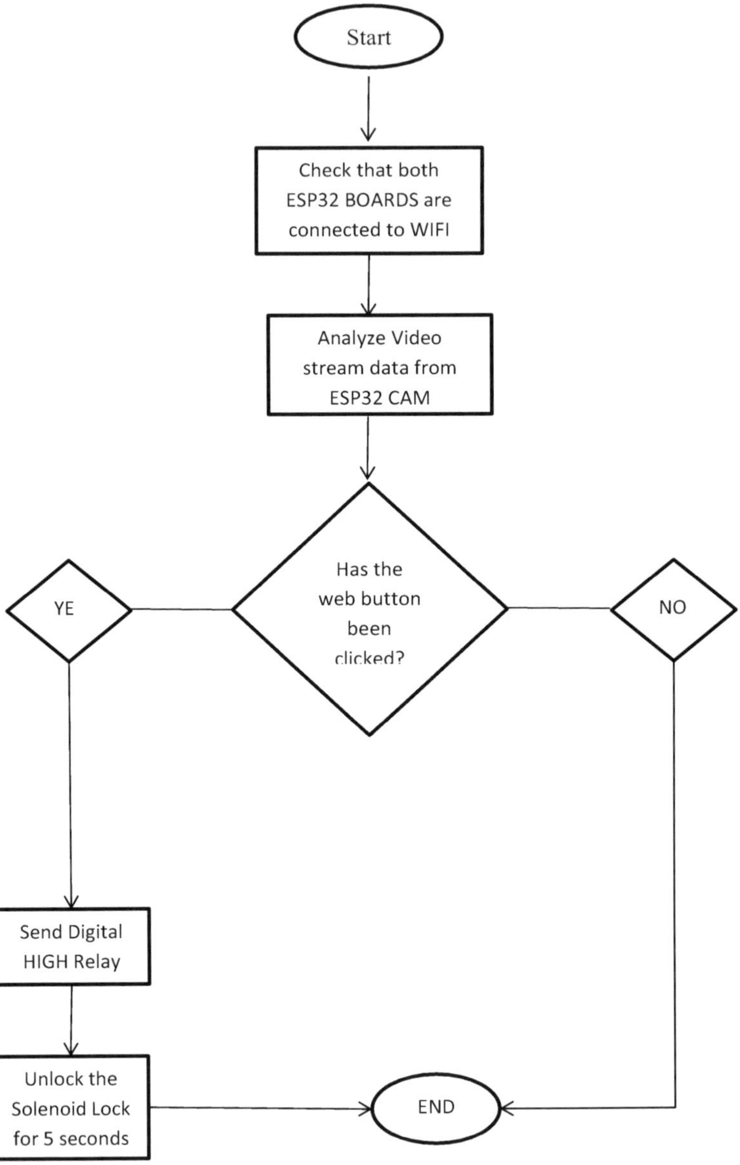

Fig. 3.11 Flow chat algorithm from which the program.

3.10 Fabrication Procedure

The IOT based access control door fabricated in this work is made using several components and materials with the door frame and door being the parent components of the system. The door and its frame are fabricated from formica particle board wood. This is done by cutting the formica spans to a desired dimension with an electric chop saw. The door frame measures 1066.8mm by 762mm with the door itself measuring 914.4mm by 609.6mm.

Formica particle board is chosen as the main material for this fabrication because of its light weight, resistance to corrosion and known strength. The cut pieces of formica particle board are then framed together by drilling holes with an electric hand drill and fastening the spans together using screws. After the frame has been made, the door material is also cut and framed using the same procedure. The door was measured to be3ft by 2ft.

A support frame and stand is fabricated using ply wood to enable the door stand on its owns. The door and its frame the are then fitted into this wooden stand and screwed to it at all four corners. The Solenoid lock, ESP32 CAM, and the control electrical circuit are then attached to complete the fabrication. The code which controls the entire system is loaded to the microcontroller and the IOT based door is ready for testing. Figure 3.16 and 3.17 reveal the fabricated system.

Fig 3.16: Front view of door design

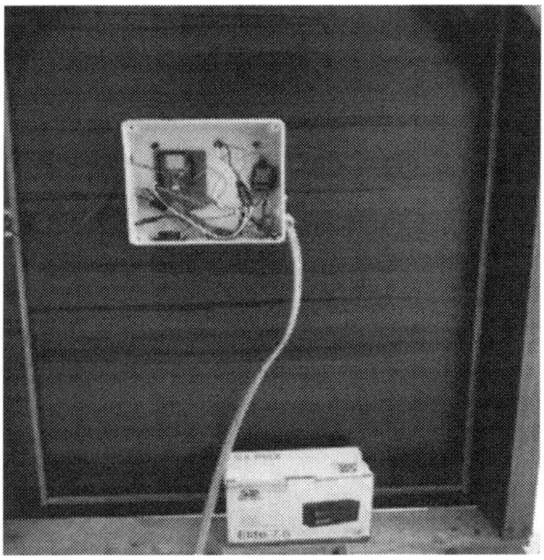

Figure 3.17: Rare view of door design

CHAPTER 4

RESULTS AND DISCUSSION

In designing the IOT based access control door, several parameters are considered. These parameters were instrumental in carrying out the engineering design calculations which informed the choice of components and materials used in the fabrication and also the design of the IOT based access control door. These parameters are shown in the tests result considered as shown. To validate the system designed and presented in this study, three hardware tests have been carried out. These tests include;

- ESP32 CAM video test
- Unlocking test; LCD display test
- Wi-Fi Test connection

4.1 Esp32 Cam Video Stream Test

The ESP32 CAM test is to validate that there are no factory errors on the manufacturing of the camera module. This test is done by uploading a default sketch through the FTDI to the camera board. The window session shown below indicates that the camera module is optimally designed and working. It also indicates that the camera is able to connect to LAN networks available and to provide video streaming requirement for the design. The ip address of the esp32 camera module was scanned and obtained, then loaded into a template camera sketch which was uploaded to the camera module. The Wi-Fi SSID and password were preset in the program such that the ESP will only connect to predefined networks and not any other networks. This is done to reduce the tendency for erroneous readings A screen session to show successful Wi-fi connection and video streaming have been provided in figure 4.1 and 4.2 respectively.

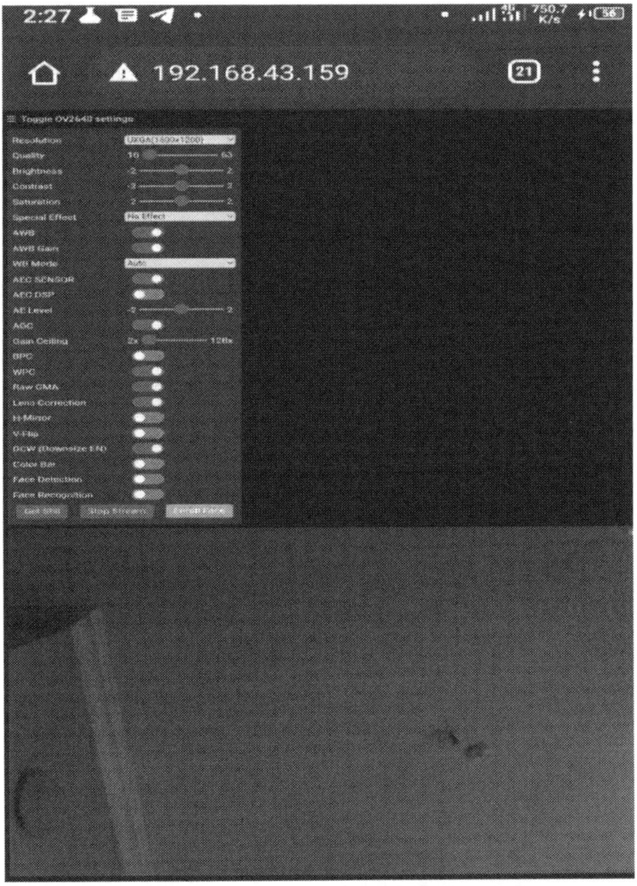

Fig. 4.1: Mobile Stream of ESP32 CAM footage

Fig. 4.2: ESP32 CAM WiFi connection Test

Asides the video stream data, there is also a generated information for the serial monitor while the streaming is going on. The serial monitor information provides the ip address that the ESP32 CAM is connected on. This serial monitor result is presented below.

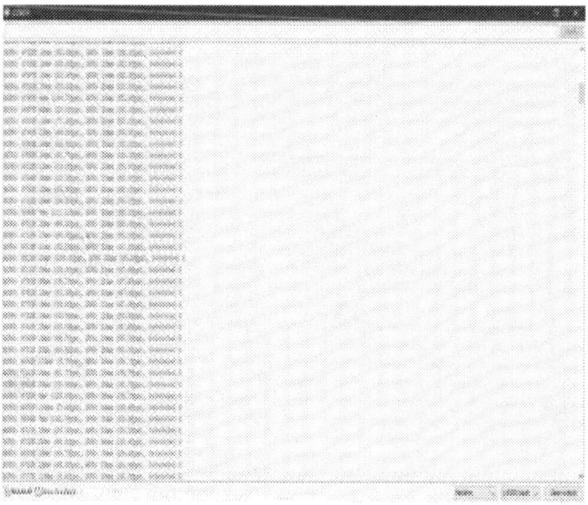

Fig. 4.3: ESP32 CAM Data Stream on serial monitor

This last test is done hand in hand with the 5V relay test since the unlocking actuator is connected to the battery source through the 5V relay modules. The LCD screen provides visual information on the status of the door at any instant of time. Images showing these tests are presented below.

4.2 Discussion

The IOT based access control door fabricated in this work, is one which uses an IP cam-the ESP32 CAM- in the viewing of activities around the door area and informing the corresponding unlocking action. From Fig. 4.4, it can be observed that when the online button is pressed, a digital HIGH is sent to the relay module which triggers it to unlock the solenoid lock whenever access is to be granted. This was done by interfacing the ESP32 MCU which is already connected to WiFi network with a 5V relay Module, and interfacing the solenoid lock to the common of the 5V relay. This is achieved when the ESP 32 receives a flag to grant access.

Due to the interfacing of the physical hardware to an IOT database, the Solenoid lock only opens when the command to open is activated online, and locks again after 10seconds of receiving a digital HIGH. Opening and closing of the door is done online requiring no one to manually unlock the door, thus making it stress-free and devoid of various constraints.

CHAPTER 5

CONCLUSION AND RECOMMENDATIONS

5.1 Conclusion

The system which is the design and fabrication of an IOT based access control door was designed considering some factors such as economy, Locking mechanism, ease of operation, availability of components and research materials, efficiency, compatibility, portability and also durability. The performance of the system after test met design specifications. The general operation of the system and performance is dependent on the authorization given from the web correspondence system to the Alerting/Actuation unit. The system was designed and fabricated using ESP32 microcontroller, ESP32 CAM microcontroller, an FTDI programmer, a 5V Relay Module, a 12V Battery bank, and a Solenoid lock. The door is fabricated using formica particle board, and the stand made of plywood.

The solenoid door lock is meant to open once a flag is sent from the web correspondence system if access is to be granted. The door stays locked until the condition of a digital HIGH is met. Also the operation is dependent on the program uploaded to the microcontroller which controls the entire system. The IC's and other circuit components were soldered properly to ensure that performance of the entire system was optimal. The construction was done in such a way that it makes maintenance and repairs an easy task and affordable for the user should there be any system breakdown. All components to be soldered were soldered on one Vero board which makes troubleshooting easier. In general, the system was designed, and the real time implementation was done using the fabricated system. An LCD screen was employed to show the status of the door at any given instant of time.

5.2 Recommendations

Although the IOT based access control door designed and fabricated in this project was able to satisfy its intended aim and objectives, there still exist room for improvements in future works. We therefore suggest the following recommendations:

i. A battery charger circuit should be incorporated to ensure that the battery powering the door is always charged.
ii. The system should be made completely reliant on solar energy.
iii. A counter system should be incorporated to count the number of persons entering and existing from the door. This will ensure that the number of persons present in the building where an IOT based access control door is installed are always known.
iv. The use of only IOT based access granting should be incorporated with Biometric methods such as finger print or retina scans and access cards also.

REFERENCES

Adewuyi, P. A., Okelola, M. O. and Jemilehin, A. O. (2013). "PIC based model of an intelligent gate controller," *International Journal of Engineering and Advanced Technology,* vol. 2, pp. 601-605, 2013.

Alkar, A. Z., and Buhur, U. (2005), "An Internet Based Wireless Home Automation System for Multifunctional Devices", *IEEE Consumer Electronics, 51*(4), pp. 1169-1174.

Ashis, M., and Aman, A. (2014). Modeling & Testing of Automatic Pneumatic Sliding Door Using Sensors & Controllers. *International Journal of Scientific and Research Publications*, 4(10), October 2014. 1 ISSN 2250-3153 www.ijsrp.org

Butler, C. (1991). "Gate support and operating mechanism," ed: Google Patents.

Chai, F. S. (2009). "Design of automatic gate mechanism," *Universiti Malaysia Pahang.*

Ciubotaru-Petrescu, B., Chiciudean, D., Cioarga, R., & Stanescu, D. (2006), "Wireless Solutions for Telemetry in Civil Equipment and Infrastructure Monitoring", *3rd Romanian-Hungarian Joint Symposium on Applied Computational Intelligence (SACI)* May 25-26, 2006.

Conte, G., and Scaradozzi, D. (2003), "Viewing home automation systems as multiple agents systems", *RoboCUP2003*, Padova, Italy. http://www.robosiri.it/ROBOCUP_2003/ROBOCUP-SITOSIRI/articles/pdf/Conte.pdf.

Edward, S. and Danford,S.G. (1993). “Automated Doors: Towards Universal”, The Center for Inclusive Design and Environmental Access School of Architecture and Planning SUNY/Buffalo, USA, October 25,1993

"Front Doors, Garage Doors Insights from The Door Zone". The Door Zone. 2017-05-07

Garvin, S. (1997). "Automatic door and window controls," *Building Services Journal,* vol19, pp. 37-42,

Garvin, S. (1997). Domestic automatic doors and windows for use by elderly and disabled people: a guide for specifiers: *Construction Research Communications,* 1997.

Home Safety Guidelines for Architects & Builders, NBS GCR 78-156, BOSTI, December 1978

Horton, H. D. (1969) "Automatic gate device," ed: Google Patents, 1969.

Howard, R. T. (1997), *Science in Medieval Islam: An Illustrated Introduction*, p. 181, University of Texas Press, ISBN 0-292-78149-0.

Jonathan, A.E., and Michael, N.T. (2014) An electronically controlled automatic security access gate. *Leonardo Journal of Sciences,* 2014(25): p. 85-96.

Kalpakjian, (2008). Automation in Manufacturing. *Manufacturing processes for Engineering Materials*, 5th Ed., Pearson Education, http://nd.edu/~manufact/MPEM%20pdf_files/Ch14.pdf

I Kings 31-35. The Holy Bible. King James Version.

Mgbenu, E.N., Inyang, A.E., Agu, M.N., Osuwa, J.C., Ebong, I.D.U. (2006). Thermal Radiation. *Modern Physics*. Spectrum Books Limited, Ibadan. 2nd Edition. pp37. ISBN-10:978-029-638-7.

Needham, J. (1986). *Science and Civilization in China: 4(2), Mechanical Engineering*. Taipei: Caves Books, Ltd.

Nicholson, P. (1841). The New and Improved Practical Builder. London: Thomas Kelly. pp. 97–98.

O'brien, J. R. (2006). "Fence and method of producing such," ed: Google Patents, 2006.

Openers P. D. (2006). "Private Door Information," *Lombard", IL. http://www. private door. com,* 2006.

Patil, S. P., Dhabuwala, J. R.and Patel, L. A. (2006). "Automatic Sliding Window."

Parsadayan, W. (2000). "Safety gate operator which prevents entrapment, and method of its operation," ed: Google Patents, 2000.

Primus, C. K., Yahya, N.S., Arbai, A., Dandang, N. A. N., and Afi, N. O.(2015). Design and Development of Low Cost Auto Gate System for House, Part 4. *2nd Integrated Design Project Conference (IDPC) Faculty of Mechanical Engineering, Universiti Malaysia Pahang*, 11 Dec 2015. 1.

Texas Instruments (2016). L293x Quadruple Half-H Drivers. L293, L293D. Texas Instruments Incorporated. www.ti.com

Zungeru, A. M. and Abraham-Attah, P. O. (2013). A Digital Automatic Sliding Door with a Room Light Control System. https://www.researchgate.net/publication

Publisher: Eliva Press Global Ltd

Email: info@elivapress.com

Made in United States
Orlando, FL
04 November 2026

90209051R00033